JOURNEY TO ABUNDANCE™ SERIES

THE
VISION
THING

The first step on your organization's

journey to abundance

THE

VISION

THING

The first step on your organization's

journey to abundance

ISBN 978-1-365-91811-7

Copyright © 2009

This printing/edition August 2017

The Telein Group, Inc.

www.telein.com

Phone 001 714.952.4444

CONTENTS

ABOUT THIS GUIDE

"They say that when there is no Vision, the people perish. But give those same people a Vision of the wonderful future that could be theirs, and everything they touch begins to thrive and grow."

Anonymous

AS A LEADER, YOU WANT TO MAKE YOUR MARK, to lead your people to a higher level, to improve your results, and to leave a positive legacy. You want to see improvement and change in all areas of your organization – including in yourself and your team.

At Telein, our firm belief is that, these goals are not only attainable, but they're just the tip of the iceberg. We believe in (and have the expertise to help you envision and create) results that are abundant, sustainable and repeatable, for yourself as an individual and for your organization.

Nevertheless, with the many demands and pressures coming from every direction, it can be tough to separate yourself from the constant pull of the day-to-day and focus on

---

clarifying your goals for the organization's future. It can be even more difficult to consistently lead with that future in mind and to engage others in the same direction.

Yet, without the clarity that comes from thinking deeply about your dreams for yourself and your organization, the end result will be a frustrating, vicious cycle where actions eventually reveal themselves to be no more than random activities, disconnected from a meaningful goal. And without a process to engage and involve all of the stakeholders above and below you, inside and outside of your organization, you will end up feeling like a salmon swimming upstream while the organizational current runs in the opposite direction.

Based on our three decades of working with organizations around the world, The Telein Group, Inc. has developed processes to enable leaders to move from a paradigm of reacting and fighting the fires of today to one where they proactively, purposefully and interdependently create the abundant future they desire for themselves and their organizations. It's a journey requiring discipline, commitment and change, with spectacular results as the payoff. Clarifying and documenting your vision of the future is the first step on that journey.

This guide has been written for organizational leaders regardless of size, industry or field of endeavor. It explains the what, why, who and how of writing an effective Vision, and outlines our process to identify, articulate and begin to pursue your vision, thus leading your organization to that higher level.

As you read, take notes of things that speak to you, and ideas that come to your mind. Vision is the result of deep thought about yourself, your values, your goals, and your environment. When you put down this guide and go about your work and your life, keep your eyes and ears open for words, ideas and situations that speak to you and give you fodder for your Vision. Jot them down, clip them out, and keep them together.

Writing a Vision is the beginning of a journey that is proactive, purposeful and transformational, and one that will require discipline, commitment and change. It is a journey that must engage the head, heart and hands of all stakeholders, whether they be customers, employees, families, or communities.

The payoff will be the achievement of the spectacular and sustainable results you want for your organization, and the realization of your deeply-held and abundant dream.

THE VISION THING

WHAT IS A VISION AND WHY DO I NEED ONE?

"Significant Vision precedes significant success."

Joel Barker

WHAT IS A VISION?

A Vision is a picture of the future you desire. It is a description of your organization's ideal state, five to ten years from now. It describes where you want to go and how you'll get there. It provides a framework for change and for action. It is aspirational and inspirational, and has a message for everyone who is involved with or affected by the Vision. It is a description of your superordinate, overarching goal.

A Vision is multi-faceted. It describes the desired outcomes the organization seeks to achieve. It also describes the ways in which people's lives, both within and outside of the organization, benefit from this Vision being fulfilled.

More than any other factor, Vision shapes your reality. To stay relevant, contributing and thriving, you must have a Vision of your organization as such. You must define what relevant, contributing and thriving looks like in your particular situation, so that you can create yourself in that mold. Having and holding a clear Vision as your goal is necessary, no matter the size or type or organization.

You need a Vision whether your organization is a large business or an entrepreneurial start-up, a university or a classroom, a non-profit or a church, a sports team or a family. Whenever and wherever people come together united by a common purpose, Vision is clarifying, unifying and motivating.

In this guide, the term "organization" is used in a broad sense, to mean a group of people who "organize" themselves into a unit of any size, for any purpose. It encompasses business organizations, educational organizations, governmental organizations, etc. It also refers to organizations within organizations, such as departments or teams.

Whatever their size or purpose, organizations often seem complex, with multiple people, pieces, and processes. Yet, no matter how large an organization may be, all of those parts and pieces can be reduced to just two things, which represent, fundamentally, what an organization is: **purpose** and **relationships**.

The purpose is the goal, the vision, the reason the organization exists. The relationships are the people, the processes, how they work together, what they produce, how they interact, overlap and interrelate.

An organization, then, can be thought of simply as **"multiple people with a common goal"** – or, put another way, "relationships with purpose." Every action that takes place in an organization takes place *because of* the purpose and *through* the relationships.

The first person who will benefit from your Vision is you, the leader. Determining your Vision will give you the focus, clarity

---

and direction you need to lead effectively. Having a clear, thoughtful, detailed end state – or Vision – for where the organization is going is imperative to connect all the "relationships" and get them thinking in an integrated fashion and moving in the same direction.

WHY DO I NEED A VISION?

Vision clarifies and articulates the goal. You may already have a good sense of your goals and values, but the process of Visioning, with the deep thinking, decision-making and documenting it requires, will help you make those goals and values crystal clear, explicit and tangible. This is of benefit, not only to you, but to everyone involved with or affected by your Vision, or your "Vision community." When everyone understands the goals in a similar way, everyone can act and choose accordingly.

Vision provides a map. The philosopher Seneca said, "If one does not know to which port one is sailing, no wind is favorable." Happily, the opposite is true for those who have a clear Vision: If you *do* know where you're going, *all* winds are favorable. That means, when you know your destination, circumstances won't prevent you from reaching it, because you can adjust your direction accordingly, and turn the situation to your advantage. When Vision is clear, the appropriate connections between relationships – whether between individuals, processes or departments – can be seen more easily and effective decisions can be made. You'll be less affected by the many distractions that inevitably appear, because your Vision guides you about how and what to choose. You can see what fits and what doesn't.

Vision creates shared meaning. Through dialogue and exposure to the Vision, a greater level of common understanding will develop amongst everyone in the Vision community. Vision serves as a clear guide for everyone, so that the actions of diverse people, with different roles, in different situations, can be connected and move in the same direction.

Vision ties actions to dreams. Vision provides motivation and direction to guide the decisions, actions and behaviors of everyone in the organization. It undergirds activity with purpose, creating a "why" for every "what." The inspiration, information, accountability and challenge found in the Vision provide an integrated, consistent framework for the behavior and decisions of each person in the Vision community.

Vision ignites the human spirit. Human beings are hard-wired to strive in the direction of goals. From the time you get up in the morning until you lay down at night, your life is a series of mini-goals, first envisioned and then achieved. You get up with a goal to get dressed, a goal to complete a certain task at work, a goal to prepare a meal. You have bigger goals, which take far more than a minute or a day, but everything you do, before it becomes a reality, exists in your mind as a goal. Whether your goals are small or large, your reality bends towards them.

When you write a Vision, you make goals that are big and broad. And when you share that Vision with others, you ignite the power within everyone in your organization, and multiply your chances of making Vision a reality.

THE DIFFERENCE BETWEEN A VISION AND A MISSION

A vision statement is different from a mission statement, although both play an important role in articulating the purpose of an organization.

We advocate that an effective **VISION** is a detailed, comprehensive, inspiring description of your desired end point. The organization's Vision is created by the leader, and shared with everyone in the organization for understanding and support. It is like a lighthouse in the distance, providing light and clarifying direction. Vision is a broad, all-encompassing description of your organization in the future.

Your organization's **MISSION**, on the other hand, is focused and specific. It describes who you are, what you do, for whom, and why. It should be developed by all the people whose responsibility it will be to carry it out. For example, an organization's specific mission should be defined by the Leadership or Executive Team. Your Mission is the "bull's eye" of your broader Vision.

A Vision is a description of a different future reality. It is a description of change. But making desired change a reality is challenging, and we agree with Harvard professor Michael Beer, who says that overcoming the many and varied hindering factors to change requires three things: a **Desire** to change, a **Model** for change, and a **Process** to change.

You may already have the necessary **Desire** for yourself and your organization to change, but you may not yet have determined what that change should be. A detailed Vision provides you with the **Model** for what you want your change to look like. It will provide you with the focus, clarity and direction you seek. And, writing an effective Vision is the first of four-steps in our proven organization transformation **Process** – the Telein Journey© Process.

The Telein Journey©, illustrated simply below, is a unique, integrative process for leading and managing whole system, transformative organizational change. The process begins with a Vision, is initiated by the leader, is facilitated by a Telein advisor, and requires the meaningful involvement of everyone in the organization. The Journey's stages and processes integrate and overlap to harness not only the power of Vision, but also the power of people, spirit, process and dialogue in the direction of results that are guaranteed to be sustainable, repeatable and spectacular.

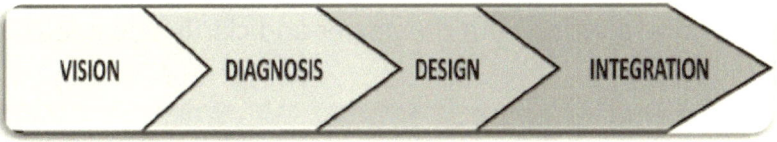

VISION · DIAGNOSIS · DESIGN · INTEGRATION

WHAT ARE THE QUALITIES OF AN EFFECTIVE VISION?

"Dreams are the seedlings of reality."

James Allen

TO INSPIRE AND GUIDE YOURSELF AND OTHERS to move in a new direction, your Vision must have power. A goal that is too easily achieved or ordinary won't provide motivation. Your Vision must be clearly stated, because if it is too short or vague, it is open to interpretation. The following four qualities of an effective Vision, developed by Joel A. Barker, are a framework for creating a Vision with the power and clarity you need.

AN EFFECTIVE VISION IS LEADER-INITIATED

The Vision must come from the leader, as they are the only one who has both the authority and the influence to determine the direction for the organization, and to unite that direction with the relationships of the organization, so that everyone and everything works together, toward one goal. By creating and leading with a Vision for your organization, you provide motivation and direction for yourself and others. By clearly sharing your Vision, inviting everyone to participate and providing the needed tools and processes, you bring purpose and relationships together.

Your organization is a reflection of you, and will never be more effective than you. Having an honest, accurate understanding of yourself – your values, beliefs, dreams, strengths, weaknesses – is a critical first step toward clarifying and articulating your Vision for the organization.

When you develop your Vision consistent with who you are as an individual, you will be better able to lead towards it with the courage, conviction and resolve that will be required. When you focus on knowing and growing yourself, you'll be better able to lead and grow your organization. You will become the champion your Vision requires.

AN EFFECTIVE VISION IS POSITIVE AND INSPIRING

Not only must the Vision connect deeply with you as the leader, but, to gain the necessary commitment from all the people throughout the organization, the Vision must make a connection with them as well. In order for people to join you in pursuit of the Vision, they need to see it as worthwhile, desirable and compelling.

People have an innate desire to do work that is meaningful and to make a contribution that is valuable. A positive, inspiring Vision connects with this innate human desire and acts like a magnet, drawing people to participate with enthusiasm in its pursuit.

Vision must represent a significant, positive change from the status quo. It shouldn't be a goal that is easily reached, but should represent a challenge, requiring commitment, energy and determination from everyone. It's better to set the bar too high, and err on the side of too great a vision, because when people are inspired and involved, they will rise to the challenge every single time. It is when people are not given the opportunity to participate meaningfully in something worthwhile, that they become bored and apathetic.

Individually and collectively, the human spirit is inspired and ignited by goals that are very big, particularly when they can be pursued in collaboration with other people. A Vision that requires stretch, growth and change on the part of the people who are making it happen, for the sake of a lofty goal and abundant results for all concerned, is worth the effort.

AN EFFECTIVE VISION IS COMPREHENSIVE AND DETAILED

To become engaged, people must be able to see themselves in the Vision. They need to see how they will participate and contribute in a meaningful way, how they are important and

---

significant in the Vision, as well as how they will benefit from it. The Vision, therefore, should cover every aspect of the organization, every function's unique and important role. It must be "a picture of the future with everyone in it" and provide information that is applicable to every person, in every role, in the organization.

The Vision cannot be simply a short statement or paragraph, something that will be reduced to merely a slogan or elevator speech, or pinned to a bulletin board. It must become a living document that provides a framework for answers for everyone in the organization. When people are in doubt about what to do or how to do something in their work, they should be able to find direction by asking, "What does the Vision say?" Such a Vision becomes a principle-based guide for daily use, far more useful than any policy manual or set of rules. In this way, Vision replaces supervision.

Your Vision should be a comprehensive, detailed description of your organization 5-10 years from now. Depending on your organization and situation, a sufficiently comprehensive and detailed Vision may be between 20 and 50 pages long. Thinking and writing in such detail takes effort, yet it will pay incredible dividends when you're able to use your Vision to guide your actions every day and see others doing the same.

AN EFFECTIVE VISION IS SHARED AND SUPPORTED

Some organizations produce a Vision statement, post it on the wall, send it out in a newsletter, and then are surprised when things fail to change. That's because creating a Vision is only the very first step of what needs to be done to turn it into reality. As the leader, you can and should determine and write your organization's Vision yourself, but you cannot make it a reality all by yourself.

You know that if you could just get everyone in the organization moving in the same direction, that you would succeed, whatever your goal. Well, the first step towards being able to move in the same direction is letting everyone know, very clearly, what that direction is.

Thus, the Vision you create must be shared with every single person in the organization. Furthermore, it must be understood by everyone, which means that, beyond hearing and reading the Vision, people need the opportunity to interact with it and talk about it. They need the opportunity to ask questions and dialogue amongst themselves and with you.

Gaining a broad and shared common understanding of the Vision throughout the organization provides the foundation for the commitment and support that will be needed. To quote author and personal effectiveness guru Stephen Covey, *"no involvement, no commitment."* Consistent and meaningful involvement and communication will yield abundant results.

WHAT ARE THE COMPONENTS OF AN EFFECTIVE VISION?

"Vision determines your destination

because reality bends to your dreams."

LIKE A WELL-TOLD STORY, A VISION REQUIRES CERTAIN ELEMENTS to make it effective, to connect with the reader, and to make a compelling case for your new direction. Following are the components, or pieces, which every Vision should have.

COMPONENTS OF AN EFFECTIVE VISION

1. INTRODUCTION & HISTORY

2. VISION END POINT

3. CULTURE

4. CORE CAPABILITIES

5. CLOSING & EXPECTATIONS

1. INTRODUCTION & HISTORY

The *Introduction* sets the stage for the details that are to come, anchoring readers with a similar perspective. In the Introduction, context for the Vision is given. Outline your current organizational setting and situation. Mention factors or shifts in the world around you, such as societal, political or global trends. These factors are the context in which you've reconsidered your direction. If you belong to a larger organization that already has a broader Vision, then that is part of your context as well.

An essential part of the introductory section of your Vision is a review of the *History* of your organization. Looking back reminds you and others of how and why your organization got to where it is today. It will often connect you with deep values or ideas which may have faded or been forgotten, but provide important clues to where to go from here. It is also a way to acknowledge and appreciate the thinking and efforts that have gone before, and connect your future journey to your past one, rather than separate yourself from it.

Additionally, it can be very insightful, both to yourself and others, to reflect on and write about your personal history, particularly if your organization is a new or small and personal one. Your unique, individual background, life and career experiences, and beliefs and values are part of the root system of the Vision you are about to write. Sharing something about them provides a deeper, more meaningful way to connect with your readers and organizational members.

2. VISION END POINT

The Vision End Point is like a "snapshot" of your desired future state. It is an overall, comprehensive yet condensed summary of the Vision in action. It describes your organization when your Vision is achieved.

The Vision End Point is the big picture of your realized Vision, providing the foundation and framework for all the details to come. The compelling picture it depicts acts like a magnet, attracting the mindset and behaviors you will need.

The Vision End Point describes (in present tense, as though it were already a reality) the outcomes, or tangible results of achieving your Vision. What have we accomplished? How do we do things? What are we good at? What are the keys to our success? How do we behave? What are we known and admired for? What do others, outside of our organization, say about us? How have we improved the lives of ourselves and others?

3. CULTURE

The *Culture* section describes the "how" of your high-performing, abundant organization. It describes in detail "the way we do things around here." Culture springs from values and beliefs shared throughout the organization and provides the foundation for all the work of the organization, and for realizing the Vision End Point. In effect, your organization's culture represents the "head, heart and hands" of the organization's people, as it is a description of the way everyone thinks, feels and, thus, behaves.

Without creating and maintaining the Culture of the Vision, the End Point cannot be realized. Culture is the glue that enables everyone to work together effectively in any situation, and becomes your organization's inimitable and differential competitive advantage.

The Culture section should describe the shared Values & Beliefs, Competencies and Behaviors of all members of your Vision community. Additionally, you may include processes and tools that are fundamental to the behavior of everyone and, thus, the Culture of the organization.

The Culture required to achieve your End Point Vision provides the foundation for the Core Capabilities you will need.

4. CORE CAPABILITIES

If Culture is "how" you do things in your organization's desired Vision state, then the *Core Capabilities* are "what" you will do. Core Capabilities are the broad strengths that will need to be in place across your organization. They are the big things at which your organization will excel.   Usually four to six such Core Capabilities are required in order to reach your End Point Vision.

The Core Capabilities underpin your organization's processes and tools, and must be developed across and throughout your organization, not just in specific areas of the organization. In the Vision document, the Core Capabilities must be identified and explained in detail.

5. CLOSING AND EXPECTATIONS

The *Closing* ties all the sections together, connecting where you're going with how you'll do things and what you'll do to get there.

In the Closing, extend an invitation to all members of your Vision community to join you on the journey. Be clear about your leadership expectations going forward. This Vision is a mandate for all involved, not merely a suggestion.

Let people know that each and every one of them is invited and welcome – in fact, is **expected** and **required** – to participate in planning for and achieving the desired End Point. Let them know they will participate in the work, and in the rewards. Let them know that they will be communicated with and involved going forward. And, importantly, let them know that the pursuit of this goal begins now.

IN SUMMARY

In summary, making Vision a reality works like the following multiplication equation:

CULTURE x CORE CAPABILITIES = END POINT VISION
how you do things   *what you're good at*   *your desired future state*

When your organization has developed a high level of expertise in each of the **Core Capabilities**, *and* when everyone is consistently behaving in the manner described in the **Culture**, the result will be the organization described in the **End Point Vision.** One or the other isn't enough. If you have broad organizational expertise without a high-performing culture, or if you have a winning culture but inadequate expertise or delivery, you will not have a sustainably successful, abundant organization. Just like a multiplication equation, if any of the factors is "zero", the equation's product becomes zero.

HOW DO I GET STARTED?

"Vision without action is merely a dream.

Action without Vision just passes the time.

*But Vision **with** action can change the world."*

Joel Barker

NOW YOU KNOW THE QUALITIES YOUR VISION NEEDS TO HAVE in order to connect with its constituents. You know the components required to make it future-focused, comprehensive and achievable. Still, creating a Vision for the future of your organization is a significant task and can be daunting. You may wonder where to begin. This section outlines the process of writing an effective Vision, in terms of the following four main steps.

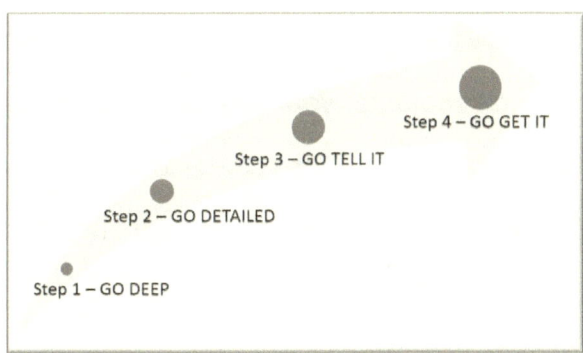

STEP ONE – GO DEEP

Reflect, Diagnose, Visualize, Dream

Vision is about change. However, it must be rooted in things that do *not* change, in order to provide an anchor and a foundation from which to build. Reflecting on the things that are at the core of you and your organization will provide you with the foundation from which to visualize and dream.

Vision doesn't come out of nowhere. The clues and cues about what your specific Vision should be are within you and all around you. They can be found in the desires and needs of yourself, your stakeholders, your world. Your job as a Vision-writer is to pay attention to those clues, to understand them, to think about how your organization's unique and important role in meeting those needs, and to focus that into a Vision.

Keep in mind that, while **you** are the expert in your organization, and **you** are the leader whose Vision is being clarified, it can be valuable to have someone with whom to dialogue, someone who will ask questions, probe, listen and challenge. A trusted confidante, mentor or advisor can be tremendously helpful in listening and providing feedback and input.

Extended blocks of time for reading, reflection, dialogue and writing are essential. You will benefit from carving out significant periods of time, and working in a place where you won't be interrupted and can make this work your priority.

Consider retreating away from your workplace or home, to somewhere apart from the fray of everyday life, perhaps to a place of beauty, peace and inspiration.

Understand yourself. Your organization and your Vision are reflections of you. Therefore, the first – and most important – thing to do is reflect deeply and honestly on yourself. Ask yourself, who am I? What are my strengths and weaknesses, my history and experiences? Visualize yourself 5-10 years from now.

Understand who you are, and accept or change yourself. Remember, your organization's growth cannot be greater than your own. In order to grow your organization, you must grow yourself.

Below are some questions and thought-starters. Think about each question, and take the time to write your answers in full sentences. The act of writing in this way gives substance and clarity to thoughts and ideas that may never have been expressed.

What are my personal strengths? My personal weaknesses? What are my history and experiences? What are my deepest beliefs? My values? My priorities? What gives me joy and satisfaction? What am I passionate about? What would I do even if it was not rewarded? What do I want to accomplish with my life? What legacy do I want to create? Why am I in this organization? Are my reasons being fulfilled? How do I want to contribute to my world? How do I want to connect with my world? How do I want to integrate the various aspects of my life? How would I describe the person I am becoming? How would I describe the person I want to become?

Understand your environment. Consider your marketplace, your customers, and all the stakeholders in your business. Consider the wider world – politics, economics, emerging trends, etc. Study similar organizations, different organizations, organizations you admire and would like to emulate. What do you admire about them? What would you emulate? What would you do differently? Continuously keep your eyes and ears open. Read broadly, highlight, make notes, clip things out and hold onto them. There will be connections and themes to the things that resonate with you.

Following are some things to think about and questions to ask yourself. Describe the environment in which you must succeed (organizationally, locally, nationally, globally). What are the changes taking place in my environment? What are the trends? What is causing these changes? What, if anything, is our ability to influence these changes? How does my organization fit into the larger organization, community, etc? How do we participate in the larger organization's achievement of its goals? How should we participate? How is my organization perceived by others (internal and external customers, etc.)? What do I think the future will hold? What are the opportunities in my current or future environment? Threats?

What are my organization's strengths in the face of these changes? Weaknesses?

Understand your organization. Where it is now, where is it going, how do the parts and pieces fit together, what are the issues, who are the people, what do they think? Spend time with the people, asking questions, working side by side, in every corner of the organization. Go where you haven't gone before. Walking around and speaking with people in the organization can yield invaluable insights leaders may otherwise miss.

There are many questions to ask yourself, which will help bring ideas to mind. What is the essence of this organization? What is its current personality? How do we need to change? What is the foundation and heritage on which we can build a better future? What is our function? How do we carry it out? How *should* we carry it out instead? How are we viewed? How do we want to be viewed instead? Inside of what bigger frameworks must we operate? What is our history? How did we get here? Why do we do the things we do? What are our current strengths? What strengths must we have in the future? What are our weaknesses? How must we change? What single words describe who/what we are now? What single words describe what we must become in our ideal future state? What organizational outcomes must we achieve? What human outcomes?

Imagine the future by tapping into both sides of your brain – the creative, intuitive right brain and the logical, verbal left brain. Visualize the essence of your organization in 5-10 years and draw a picture of it. Or, you may choose to write a poem, song or a story, if you like, or to create a collage from photos or clippings.

Any creative method that works for you is fine. The key is to get creativity flowing and tap into ideas and emotions that may not come to the surface using traditional thinking techniques. This is a powerful way to identify things you may not be able to put into words.

STEP TWO – GO DETAILED

Plan, Organize, Write

Once you've done the introspective and investigative work of reflecting on yourself and your organization, it's time to flush out the details and put it all together on paper.

First of all, the more comprehensive and detailed the Vision is, the more it will serve as a guide for yourself, and then for every person in the organization. Write as if you had your organization under a microscope and were documenting the details. Provide a framework and answers for all aspects of the organization, every function, every process, every person.

At the same time, avoid unnecessary complexity and redundancies. Like a diamond, your Vision may be elegant in its simplicity, yet it has many facets to be explored and described.

Bring the Vision to life by using stories, examples, quotes, illustrations, etc. Consider working with a professional artist or illustrator to develop customized illustrations that add meaning. This is where the hard work of "going deep" pays off.

Once the fundamentals of your Vision are in place, they are unlikely to change. However, you may decide at some point to modify certain details of your Vision based on new thoughts or input. Keep a "draft mentality" about your Vision and be open to considering modifications or improvements.

Following is additional explanation, along with questions and thought-starters. Some of the questions are reiterated in more than one place. For recommendations about an effective Vision writing style, *see the section Writing Tips near the end of this Guide.*

Vision End Point – The Big Picture

Writing about your End Point Vision provides the foundation for the details of your Vision. Describe the End Point in the present tense, as if it were already achieved.

Some questions to ask yourself as you flush out the various aspects of your Vision End Point state might include: How would I comprehensively describe the organization we have become? What are the organizational outcomes we have achieved? What are our human outcomes? What critical function do we serve for our internal and external customers? How do we perform that function with excellence? How did we become the organization we are today? How do we interact with one another and with people outside of the organization? How do we collaborate? How do we make decisions? What is

---

our reputation with all our stakeholders (e.g., customers, vendors, industry, communities, families, ourselves, etc.)? How do others outside of our organization describe us? What words describe how we feel about ourselves and our work?

Once you have the elements of this story determined, it can be very powerful and motivating to express the End Point Vision in a creative way, as though it were written from the perspective of someone outside the organization. Consider writing it as a newspaper or magazine article about your future organization, or write a script of yourself being interviewed talking about your organization's great success and how it was achieved.

Culture – Your Organization's DNA

Describe in vivid detail "what we believe, how we behave, and how we do things around here." Your **Values & Beliefs** must be at the heart of your organization's Culture, must undergird all actions and must be shared by everyone. Develop a set of

Competencies – those qualities, skills and styles that represent your Values & Beliefs.

Write the ways in which you want to see these values and beliefs lived out by everyone – including yourself – on a daily basis, in every part of the organization. Ask yourself, "How will I know the Culture when I see it? How will it be brought to life, every day, in every way?"

What values do we hold as an organization, which enable us to reach our End Point? What behaviors do we practice consistently and hold ourselves and one another accountable to? What overarching processes do we use throughout the organization, which are consistent with and reinforce our Culture?

Describe your desired organizational Culture from as many angles as you can think of – whether it be attitudes and practices regarding communication, practices and processes for decision-making, planning, teaming, legal, and financial, attitudes towards diversity and differences; and even things that seem small, such as everyday attitude, personal attire and physical appearance, and the ways people treat one another, both inside and outside of the organization.

Core Capabilities – What We're Good At

As you think about how your organization must function, and what you want to accomplish, what four to six essential broad strengths begin to emerge? What are the things at which your organization must be very good at in order to make your End Point Vision a reality?

These are your organization's broad capabilities, rather than specific skills. The Core Capabilities must be developed and applicable across and throughout the organization, not just functionally or by department. Describe the Core Capabilities the organization you envision must have in excruciating detail. Why are these capabilities critical to achieving your End Point? How have you developed them throughout the organization?

What do they look like in action? How can each of them be seen in various areas of the organization?

Remember, everyone in the organization must be able to see their important and significant place in the Vision, and understand what they need to do to participate in realizing the Vision. Describe how these Core Capabilities would look in every area of your organization.

STEP THREE – GO TELL IT

Broadly Share

Mark Twain said, "The man who does not read has no advantage over the man who cannot read." And so it is with a Vision: A leader with a vision that isn't shared is no better off than a leader with no vision at all. Vision must be broadly shared.

The Vision starts off as the leader's dream and goal, but it must become the dream and goal of everyone whose support and commitment is necessary to transform the Vision from a powerful but imaginary dream into a tangible and abundant reality. Gaining shared understanding of and commitment to the Vision is imperative in order to get everyone collectively moving towards it, and it is a process that takes time and determination.

Since an organization is nothing more than a group of individual people, it follows that there can never be organizational change without individual change. Every organization is, in reality, a reflection of its people's behavior. And, an organization that has changed and is achieving abundant results is, in reality, the cumulative result of many individuals behaving in an abundant manner.

To get that cumulative ball rolling, therefore, once you have a draft of your Vision completed, it's time to share it. If the size of your organization is small enough, gather everyone together to read and dialogue the Vision together. If your organization is large, begin by sharing with and gaining support from those closest to you, perhaps the people who report directly to you.

Take the time to share your Vision thoroughly and completely. Don't delegate the responsibility of sharing the Vision to others in the organization. You are the one with whom this dream began, and you are the one who has the necessary authority and influence. Everyone in the organization must support this Vision and participate in making it happen – but you are the leader, the visionary, the one who can best tell your story.

It is important to hear the Vision directly from you. Read it aloud, adding your own color commentary, stories and examples as you go. Give people an opportunity to talk about the Vision amongst themselves, to ask questions of you, and to provide input to you. Ask questions of them as well – thought-provoking questions that will facilitate deeper thought, reflection and internalization on the part of each person. Listen carefully to be sure that people are understanding what you meant. Since, as is so often the case in communicating, the message we intend to convey isn't the message that was received, it's important to test for understanding in as many ways as you can think of.

A great way for people to creatively internalize and express the Vision is to have them to draw a picture of what the Vision means to them.

After you've shared your Vision, you may choose to make some modifications based on people's input.

Explaining the Vision once is only a start. Reference it and explain it continually. You cannot repeat yourself too much, when you want to see a sustainable change in results. In fact, a good point to remember is this: when you are so tired of talking about your Vision that you can hardly stand it, your message may finally be *starting* to get through.

STEP FOUR – GO GET IT

Relentlessly Pursue

A Vision is not simply words on a page; its whole purpose is to be translated into action, every day in every way. In The Power of Vision film, Joel Barker says, **"Vision without action is merely a dream. Action without Vision just passes the time. But Vision with action can change the world."**

Translating your dream into everyone's reality requires that Vision be followed **with** an integrative process that involves and gains commitment from everyone, cascades through your organization, and has the breadth and depth to capture all activities. Still, leading change in the direction of your Vision will take considerable time and effort, no matter how inspirational and compelling your Vision is. And you're bound to encounter resistance from some, because there's a good deal of truth in the saying that the only person who likes change is a wet baby.

When you share a new Vision for your organization's future, you are challenging the status quo. You may be challenging those who have been successful in the organization as it is now. Many will welcome and embrace the new Vision state; others will feel anxious or threatened by it. This is **human** nature. Be prepared for different reactions ranging from eager acceptance to fence-sitting to resistance and sabotage, which may or may not be overt. Be prepared for people's readiness to embrace change to take time and dialogue. Create an environment for up-front, open, honest dialogue.

Writing a Vision is only the first step on the journey to an abundant new reality. You will need a systematic, wholistic process that provides for maximum integration of the pieces and involvement of all stakeholders. You will need to be relentless, determined, tenacious and untiring in your pursuit of your dream. You will also need to be empathetic and patient in order to gain the genuine, deep and sustainable support of your team that is critical to Vision attainment.

These qualities – along with many others, including courage, optimism and persistence – will be consistently required in healthy doses. However, your passion, conviction and clarity, along with walking your talk, will serve as an inspiration and motivation to others, and will show them how they, too, can take steps towards turning your Vision of today into everyone's abundant reality of tomorrow.

You will need to continuously communicate it in informal ways. Talk about the Vision in every conversation. Look for and explain connections between what the Vision says and people's everyday actions. Every activity in the organization must connect in some way to the goal of the Vision. Every "what" must find its "why" in the Vision, or it shouldn't be done.

Your Vision needs a champion and it must be you.

WRITING TIPS

WRITING A VISION IS VERY LIKELY TO BE DIFFERENT than the writing you ordinarily do, if you do any writing at all.

You should write in your own unique, authentic voice so that your words ring true to yourself and your readers. At the same time, challenge yourself to write in a way that's expansive, understandable and clear. A wonderful Vision in the writer's mind isn't helpful if it isn't clear to those whose understanding and support is needed to make it happen.

Although it may seem unnatural and ineffective to write in a way that is different from your usual style, keep in mind you're not writing for yourself alone, but also for the heads, hearts and hands needed to achieve this lofty goal.

Following are some tips to keep in mind while writing.

Use the present tense to create an optimistic, inspirational tone. For example, "We have the highest student achievement scores in the country" is more compelling than "We will try to improve student achievement scores."

Use inviting language that is inclusive, appealing, affirming, engaging. Descriptions should be vibrant, vivid and exciting.

Keep words, sentences and paragraphs fairly short. Newspapers and magazines often use a general guideline for sentences to be no more than a dozen words, and paragraphs to be three or four sentences.

Use active voice vs. passive voice. For example, "Our Research & Development professionals use the latest innovations and trends in our industry" is more effective and connects people to their own actions more than, "The latest innovations and trends in our industry are used."

Use headings and subheadings. These tell the reader what's coming next and break up long sections of text.

Use concrete examples to illustrate a point. "Our associates' ongoing education is important to us, thus we pay for all education to upgrade workplace skills."

Avoid clichés and jargon. "Labels let you in on the scoop" is too abstract, especially when translated into another language or used in a different culture. "Container labels tell you what's inside the package" would be more effective.

Use positive statements. Making statements in the affirmative lets people know what is desired and required of them. "Follow safe practices" is a more inviting and effective statement than "Do not follow unsafe practices."

Use graphics, pictures and models to add clarity to your explanation of key points.

ADDITIONAL READING & REFERENCE MATERIALS

Contact us for information about obtaining

any of these materials.

VIDEOS

The Power of Vision by Joel Barker (DVD available through The Telein Group, Inc. or Star Thrower Distribution, Inc.)

The New Business of Paradigms by Joel Barker (DVD available through The Telein Group, Inc. or Star Thrower Distribution, Inc.)

Start With Why: How Great Leaders Inspire Action by Simon Sinek (ted.com/talks/simon_sinek_how_great_leaders_inspire_action)

ARTICLES

Thriving On Order Inc. magazine interview with visionary entrepreneur Steve Bostic, December 1989

Building Your Company's Vision, by James C. Collins and Jerry I. Porras, Harvard Business Review, September-October 1996

Telein's 7 Principles of Highly Effective Organizations Copyright © 2009 The Telein Group, Inc.

Telein's 7 Principles for Individuals Copyright © 2011 The Telein Group, Inc.

BOOKS

The Fifth Discipline Fieldbook by Peter M. Senge et al, Doubleday, 1994

The 7 Habits of Highly Effective People by Stephen M. Covey, Simon & Schuster, 1989

Telein's 7 Principles of Highly Effective Organizations Copyright © 2009 The Telein Group, Inc.

Telein's 7 Principles for Individuals Copyright © 2011 The Telein Group, Inc.

TELEIN'S 7 PRINCIPLES OF HIGHLY ABUNDANT ORGANIZATIONS

THE FOLLOWING PRINCIPLES REPRESENT Telein's core beliefs about our world and our work, and form the tenets of all our teaching. This is the philosophy that grows out of our Vision and Mission, and undergirds all that we do, whether with our clients, in our communities or amongst ourselves.

THERE IS THE POSSIBILITY OF ABUNDANCE

We are all sources of limitless and abundant possibilities.

THERE IS POWER IN INTEGRATION

Everything in the world is part of a

unified, connected, whole system.

THERE IS POWER IN PEOPLE

The human spirit is unmatched and infinite

when it is inspired, integrated and unleashed.

THERE IS POWER IN SPIRIT

A spirit of love is a prerequisite for abundance.

THERE IS POWER IN VISION

Purpose and passion inspires,

tying the smallest of actions to the biggest of dreams.

THERE IS POWER IN PROCESS

The pathway to sustainable, abundant performance

is only possible with process.

THERE IS POWER IN DIALOGUE

Whatever the question, the answer is dialogue.

ABOUT
THE TELEIN GROUP, INC.

Founded in 1988, The Telein Group, Inc. are advisors, confidants and guides to leaders, teams and organizations across five continents. Our focus on vision, integration and abundance creates profound individual and organizational impact and results.

Our work is with leaders and organizations whose beliefs are consistent with ours, and who believe in and desire to pursue the possibility of abundance, by harnessing the power of effectively integrating these principles.

Our services include:

· The Journey© Process, used by organizations of all types and sizes, is our vision-based, whole system, integrative transformation process, proven to bring abundant individual and organizational results

· Executive Advising Services, customized and provided one-on-one to leaders at all levels in all types of organizations

· Igniting Spirit In The Workplace workshop series, featuring Working Together™, our most popular workshop focused on increasing effectiveness in communication and collaboration

Contact us for more information about how you can increase the effectiveness and abundance of your unique lifework.

www.telein.com · Phone 001 714.952.4444

Vision Integration Abundance

www.telein.com

Phone 001 714.952.4444

teleinhq@telein.com

www.ingramcontent.com/pod-product-compliance
Lightning Source LLC
Chambersburg PA
CBHW021906170526
45157CB00005B/1995